To

Tony, Debbie
and Sophie,
With all my
love
        from
            Lynn.
                xxxxxx.

THE DAWN OF SPRING

Lynn Harvey

MINERVA PRESS
LONDON
ATLANTA MONTREUX SYDNEY

THE DAWN OF SPRING
Copyright © Lynn Harvey 1998

All Rights Reserved

ISBN 0 75410 298 X

First Published 1998 by
MINERVA PRESS
195 Knightsbridge
London SW7 1RE

Printed in Great Britain for Minerva Press

THE DAWN OF SPRING

Contents

The Land of Broken Dreams

I walk through a land
Where dreams are cracked
And broken like an egg,
Where hopes and ambitions
Are broken glass
Lying shattered on a concrete floor.

I walk through a land
Where all hope is lost,
Where good times are but few,
Where the dawning of a new day
Brings not hope but terror –
Fear of what is next to come.

There is, it seems, no hope
For the people of this land.
No happiness, no prosperity,
Nothing to look forward to.
But these people never give up.
For, if nothing else,
They have good fighting spirit –
Enough to eclipse the evils
Of this dark time,
To crush the bad things underfoot,
Driving away the forces of darkness
To a place from which they cannot escape.

Dawn of a New Era

See it coming through the storm.
Watch the lightning as it strikes!
Read its meaning in the stars.
Think of it when deep in thought.
See it in the faces of the people
That you pass as you walk on by.
Reach up and touch it,
For it is here!
Watch the dying embers
Of the flames of the past.
For tomorrow shall see
The dawn of a new era.

Nightfall

In the dead of night,
When darkness falls
And the world around me is still,
I lie awake
In the comfort of my own bed,
Listening to the sound of silence,
Until, in the distance,
I hear the hooting of an owl
Hunting in the darkness.

I hear noises coming from downstairs.
Suddenly, a chink of light appears at my door.
I hear footsteps on the stairs,
Soft and gentle, yet all powerful.
Who is it?
What do they want of me?
I grip my bedclothes tightly,
Hands sweating with fear,
As the door creaks open.
The hairs on my neck stand on end –
Then, in a split second,
My tension and fear are gone.
For it is only my mother,
With my hot milky drink!

End of the World

What would I miss
If the world was to end?
If the ground on which we stand,
The very air that we breathe,
Were to be no more?

I would miss the simple things,
Like the birds singing in the trees.
I would miss my family and friends –
The good times that we had
Would be just memories,
Like playing games in the street,
Sculptures in the winter snow,
Ball games in summer.
I would miss the special times of the year,
Like birthdays, Easter and Christmas.
I would miss my trips
To places far away,
As these distant places
Would no longer exist.

I send this message
From the comfort of my own home.
A home. A life that I wouldn't have
If the world was to end.

War and Peace

A world of darkness
That goodness cannot touch
Lurks somewhere at the bottom
Of the pit of hell itself –
Where men and women
Are sent away
To play a game:
The game of war.

A game of chess,
Of good versus evil,
A game in which
The innocents are pawns,
Pawns that fly planes,
Dropping bombs on cities,
Like throwing stones into water.

On the streets of those broken cities,
Dead bodies are scattered,
With survivors scavenging for food,
Scrounging for what is left of their broken lives.
Hearts fill with hope
That the war will soon end,
That their loved ones will return home,
That the dawn of a new day
Will bring peace and happiness,
In which they can rebuild
Their shattered lives.

Fire

Fire, fire, burning bright,
In a barn at dead of night.
Mighty fire taking hold,
'Control yourself' you won't be told!
Hatred burning deep inside,
Nowhere to run, nowhere to hide.
Like a demon from hell set free,
Bringing horror for all to see.
Evil battling the forces of good –
People doing as they should.
For that fire is the evil within;
We must learn to keep it forever locked in,
Never to escape, ever again!

Storm in a Teacup

In a small coffee-shop,
Somewhere in the heart of town,
I sit by the window,
Reading my newspaper
And drinking my tea.
My thoughts turn from the newspaper
To the view outside.
Here I sit, watching the world go by.

I see tourists
Viewing the town, guide book in hand.
Their only knowledge of this place
Is words in black type
On the printed page.
Some are here to shop,
Some go sightseeing,
Some are here for both.

I see people running to and fro,
Going about their everyday lives.
Taking shelter from the heavy rain,
Women carry large bags of shopping,
With screaming children running alongside.

I watch people as they work –
Roadsweepers and builders
Clearing our towns and cities
Just to make another mess.

As the rain stops,
A young woman folds her umbrella
Before entering the shop.
She places her order and takes her seat.
I then finish my tea and pack away.
With hindsight, I realise
That, staring into her teacup,
The woman was watching me!

Memories

As the sun sets over the horizon
And day turns into night,
The air turns cold,
So cold that you can see your breath.
I sit on my bed,
Warming my hands over a mug of tea,
Casting my mind back
To my childhood days.

What glorious days they were!
Filled with fun and happiness.
The games we used to play!
Me and my friends chasing each other
Through fields and woodlands,
That wonderful feeling as we did so!
I remember feeling sure that we could run
Until the end of time.

Every Sunday,
The family used to take a picnic lunch
Down by the riverside.
On our leftovers the ducks were fed;
My sisters and I played ball games in the park.

On the way home
We'd stop for ice creams
Or fish and chips.

But, sadly, those days are gone,
Now no more
Than a distant memory.
Just thinking about it
Makes me feel old.
But I'm not old.
After all,
I'm only twenty-four!

Sunday

Sunday.
A quiet day,
A day of rest,
A time for reflection.
As I sit back in my chair,
Gazing up into a deep blue, cloudless, sky –
Nothing to do, nowhere to go –
My time is my own on Sunday.
Time to enjoy, time for pleasure,
Time to think of the good things
That happened in the week gone by.

Sunday.
A day of relaxation,
A day for me to soak away life's troubles,
In a bathtub full of steaming hot water.
A day for me to dream away those troubles,
By having an extra hour in bed.

Sunday.
A short pause in the week,
Before, of course,
The worst day – Monday – comes around!

The Joys of Autumn

As I look up
Into the deep red autumn sky,
I see birds flying
To a warmer climate.
Thus, I am reminded
That the year is almost over.

I look towards the trees and hedgerows.
Their crowning glory, once green,
Has now turned to brown.
One by one, the leaves fall,
Carried away by the wind
Or washed away by the rain.

The horse chestnut tree
Sheds its fruit.
Children come along
To take that fruit away,
Using every last morsel
In their games of conkers.

As I sit by an open fire,
Logs burning amid the glowing embers,
I watch the children having fun,
As, once again, I find myself
Looking up into that autumn sky.

Colours

My first is red,
Warm and beautiful,
The colour of love.
My second is yellow,
The colour of the sun,
The colour of the daffodils in spring.

My third is blue,
The colour of a cloudless sky.
My fourth is orange,
The colour of exotic fruits.
My fifth is green,
The colour of grass and leaves.

My sixth could be any of the above.
For they are all the colours of beauty,
The colours of nature,
The colours of the earth.

Night-Time

As I climb into my bed,
Ready to rest my weary head,
I cast aside the day gone by
And join the other dreamers there on high.
For night-time is the time to dream,
The time to dream the sweetest dreams.
Dreams of walking through forests of gold,
Dreams of forgetting that you are old.
Dreams of waters crystal clear,
Dreams of having someone near.
Someone to love, to cherish, to hold,
Someone for whom to be brave and bold.
Dreams come in shapes, to twist and bend,
But soon, however, my dreams must end.
For night-time must end and morning must come:
Another day has just begun!

The Dawn of a New Day

The first hint of blue appears in the black night sky,
Ushering in the dawn of a new day.
The sun, slowly rising over the hilltops,
Makes the moon and stars, one by one, fade away –
Telling the world that the night has ended
And morning has begun.
Flowers open, and birds begin their morning song,
As the sky slowly turns from the darkness of night,
Into the bright colours
Of this wonderful new day –
A day which will go down in my memory
As one of the best of my life!

The Calm After The Storm

I'm sitting by my fire,
Mug of tea in hand,
Soft music playing in the background,
As I watch the sun
Setting in stormy skies.

I hear a clap of thunder,
Then the rain starts to pour,
Lashing down from the sky,
Hitting the concrete ground with a splash!
Tiny droplets of water,
Clear like crystal,
Colourful like a rainbow,
Trickle down my window pane,
Glittering in the bright neon lights.
I curl up in my warm and cosy bed,
Feeling at peace with myself,
Safe from nature's wrath,
Watching from a distance
As she unleashes her fury on the world outside.

The next day I take an early morning walk.
The sun has risen, the rain has stopped.
But the sweet scent of musk that it leaves behind
Is for me an experience never to be forgotten.
For the sweet smell of the night rain,
The calm after the storm,
Is truly heaven sent!

Winter Warmth

I watch the snow as it falls,
Covering the ground with a crisp, white blanket,
Feeling warm in my safe little haven.

Outside, it is cold.
The children are warmly wrapped up.
I watch them playing happily in the snow;
Memories of my own childhood come flooding back.
I relax, sit back and smile
As I take a walk down Memory Lane.

I remember the fun that we had,
My friends and me engaging one another in combat.
I remember riding down the hillside on my little wooden
sledge –
Memories of Christmases past.
Excited, I would creep downstairs,
Eagerly anticipating the wonders that awaited me.
But Winter isn't always cold, you know!
Nor is it sad,
For thinking of the good times
Can make you happy, safe and warm.

These calm and happy feelings
Warm the cockles of my heart
Against the bitterness of the cold outside.

The Sky at Night

Eclipsing the light of day
Like a shadow covering the land
Falls a thick blanket, dark and mysterious
Yet ablaze with light from the moon and stars –
Stars that burn millions of miles away,
Adding a touch of wondrous beauty
To the sky at night.

The full moon shines
In all its majestic glory.
It's nothing to be afraid of,
Strange though it may seem,
For that great silver ball
That lights up the night sky
Holds many mysteries and wonders.
We mustn't dwell too much on the bad things:
Think only of good.
But there, however, my dreams must end,
For I must return to my bed.

My Garden

In my garden grows an apple tree,
Its fruit the juiciest of apples.
Frogs hop in and out of my garden pond,
Happily playing with each other.
My garden produces the cream of the crop –
Nothing but the very best!

Winter may leave it looking lifeless and dull,
But in spring my garden comes alive!
Alive to the sound of birdsong,
My garden is ablaze with colour,
Becoming the most beautiful garden in the world,
With every single flower bursting into bloom,
Blossom growing upon the trees.

The sight of a butterfly
Sweeping gracefully across the garden
Adds to the beauty of the landscape.
How lucky I am,
To think that something so beautiful
Actually belongs to me!

Mist

Mist, mist, grey and mysterious –
What lies behind this blanket of grey
That blocks the landscape from my eyes?
What secrets does it hold,
This blanket that comes in from the sea?

Mist, mist, shielding beauty from my eyes –
Walking through the morning mist
Is like walking through a beautiful silver cloud
Into the land of nowhere:
A vast expanse of greyness,
A place where nothing exists
Except for me, myself!

The Puzzle of Life

Life is what you make it,
Or so they say,
But not for me.
I wanted so much,
But I got so little.
I wanted so much
To be like everyone else,
But fate, it seems, had other plans for me.

In the beginning,
When I first found out
The meaning of my life,
I wanted to shut myself away from it,
To go into a room, lock the door
And throw away the key,
Building an invisible wall
Between me and the rest of the world.
But I'm strong.
Spiritually, I'm a fighter.
I stood face to face with the bad times,
Tackling them head-on!

My life has certainly been no bed of roses.
But, although the good times have been few,
I can still look back and smile;
I've made what I could of my life
In spite of my problems.

It may have been a rough ride,
But at the moment
My life is running as smoothly as it can.
Lately, things have started going right for me.
I find I am now at peace with myself,
The happiest I've ever been.
My life won't always be like this.
The bad times will happen again
But when they come I'll be ready once again,
And at least I'll be able to look back and smile.

Bubbles

Bubbles, bubbles, flying high,
Flying so high I cannot reach,
Over land and over sea,
Over woods and over forests,
Hills and mountains,
Rivers and streams.

Floating through storms,
Into the warmth and calm that follows;
Floating through the night,
Into the light of a new day.
Beautiful colours, swirling around
Within their protective spheres,
Colours and spheres with lives of their own.
Yet where they will end,
Nobody knows.

Anger

It strikes from nowhere, out of the blue,
Like lightning streaking across stormy skies,
Creating havoc, causing a fire –
The flames erupt, my anger flares!
Soon it boils out of control.
It explodes engulfing all
That happen to stand in its way!
But wait a minute.
What's that I hear?
A crack of thunder,
Like a whiplash in the sky,
Commanding the clouds to burst.
The rain starts to pour,
Soon putting out the fire of my anger.
I then find that I can control
This anger within me after all!

The Autumn Sky

As I watch the sun
Setting in the autumn sky,
Its rays reach out like a hand,
Touching the clouds with a tint of gold.

That same golden hand
Brushes the leaves on the trees,
Giving the beauty of the land
That extra bit of warmth and colour –
Taking the beauty I see before me
Into a whole new dimension.

Absent Minds

As I seat myself at my desk,
In the comfort of
My humble but homely dwelling-place,
With pencil and paper in hand,
My thoughts turn towards the window.
Idly watching the world going by –

The fast, headlong pace of life.
As the traffic on the road outside
Fills the air with thick, heavy fumes,
I see men and women at work
Or, with children, doing the weekly shopping.

I see a mother with her two boys,
As she opens the door.
The boys run excitedly from the house
To climb into a waiting car.
But where they are going,
Nobody knows.

I see two dogs
Chasing each other, playing happily,
Racing along the pavement,
As happy as only dogs can be.

As my dream ends,
My thoughts return to the task in hand.
But, try as I might,
I cannot remember
Why I was sat at my desk with pencil and paper:
What was I supposed to be doing?

The Mystery of Time

From the moment we are born,
The clock never stops ticking;
From our first day at school
At the age of five,
To our last
At the age of sixteen;

From our first working day,
To the first wage packet
At the end of that week;
From our first born
To our last;
From watching them grow up,
Repeating this cycle
Over and over again.

As each year goes by,
We watch our children grow up
To have children of their own.
Seeing them makes us think back
To when we ourselves were young,
Saying to ourselves:
Where have all those years gone?

Dreams

In the dead of night,
When everything is still,
When the only sound
Is the sound of silence,
So quiet that you could hear a pin drop,
I retire to my bed,
For that is the time to dream.

I dream of flying
High above the clouds
At the speed of light.
I dream of far-off places,
Warm, with friendly people,
Or cold places
Of hatred and fear.
But nothing too bad will happen.
After all, it's only a dream.

I dream of fairy tales,
Of wishing on a star
And that wish coming true.
I dream of Cinderella
Going to the ball
In a beautiful satin dress.

I dream of ruling the world.
For if I were queen,
The world would be a happier place;
Man and Nature would live in harmony,
And all would be good in the world.

I dream of floating in a sea of colours.
One by one
I pick those colours out:
Red, green, blue and pink.

I dream of warmth and sunshine
As I walk through my field of dreams.
I dream of swimming
Through warm, calm, clear waters,
But when I reach the shores of consciousness
My night's adventures end.
For I must prepare myself
To face the day ahead.

Springtime

Daffodils are yellow,
As bright as a meadow
Where cows graze
And corn grows.
Birds are busy,
Building their nests
And laying their eggs.
Sea is green.
Trees come back to life again.

New lambs are born
And flowers bloom.
Blossoms grow
Upon the trees.
I wander about
In the countryside,
And think
Why should winter come,
When spring is so wonderful?

Susie

Picking my way through dense shrubs,
I slowly make my way into the open.
Cool, crisp, clean air with a chill wind,
Blows harshly into my face,
Making my eyes water,
But my cheeks are aglow.
Shivering, I wrap my coat tightly around my body,
Hugging myself to keep warm.
In the distance, I see a tiny white figure
Running towards me.
'Susie!' I call out her name.
She bounds over, her tail wagging as she greets me,
For Susie is my dog and my very best friend –
We do everything together!
But now it is time to leave the coldness
Of the great outdoors in autumn,
And go back home to warmth and comfort.

Beauty

Beauty is all of the good things in life,
Like childhood memories
Of warm sunny days –
Days when the family would take a picnic to the park.
We'd take scraps of food
With which to feed the ducks;
We'd watch them swim in waters
That were glittering in the sunlight.
Beauty is that special doll that I played with as a child.
Time, of course, has passed by since,
Yet she still looks beautiful,
Even now.

Beauty is walking through fields of gold,
Watching children playing games,
Hearing their screams of delight.
Beauty is watching the world in spring –
Mother Nature at her best
With flowers opening and trees waking from their long
winter's sleep.
Beauty is a wonderful feeling –
Seeing the smile on the face of a child
Receiving gifts of love.
If only everything were as beautiful as this,
The world would indeed be a wonderful place.

Love

Love is special.
Love is shared.
Love is everywhere –
There's plenty to be had.

Love is a feeling,
A bond between father and son,
Mother and daughter,
Husband and wife.

Love is strength.
Love is supporting someone in their hour of need,
No matter how heavy our burden.
Love is giving.
Love is joy.
Love is for making our world a happier place,
For if it were not for love
The world would be a cold and bitter place.